HAL•LEONARD®
VIOLIN PLAY-ALONG

AUDIO ACCESS INCLUDED

Piazzolla TANGOS

CONTENTS

To access audio visit:
www.halleonard.com/mylibrary

Enter Code
3307-8762-2224-8365

ISBN 978-1-4803-9365-3

BOOSEY & HAWKES

AN IMAGEM COMPANY

DISTRIBUTED BY

HAL•LEONARD®
CORPORATION

7777 W. BLUEMOUND RD. P.O. BOX 13819 MILWAUKEE, WI 53213

Visit Hal Leonard Online at
www.halleonard.com
www.boosey.com

Violin, Jerry Loughney

Keyboards and Percussion, Dan Maske

Cello, Angela Schmidt

Recorded and Produced by Dan Maske

Ausencias

Astor Piazzolla

Chanson de la naissance

(from Famille d'artistes)

Astor Piazzolla

Libertango

Astor Piazzolla

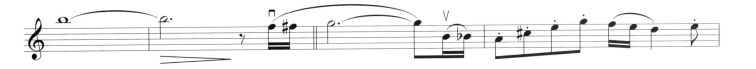

7

Los sueños

Astor Piazzolla

Sensuel

Astor Piazzolla

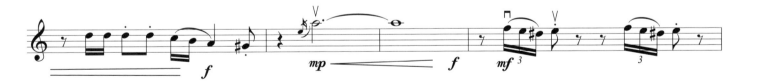

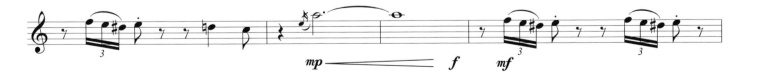

Tango apasionado

Astor Piazzolla

Vuelvo al sur

Astor Piazzolla

La chanson du Popo

(from Famille d'artistes)

Astor Piazzolla